SAVING BEAUTY
Cardinal Martini's Vision for
the New Millennium

CARLO-MARIA MARTINI
Cardinal Archbishop of Milan

Saving Beauty

Cardinal Martini's Vision for
the New Millennium

ST PAULS

Original Title: *Quale Bellezza Salvera il Mondo?*
Pastoral Letter 1999-2000
Translated from the Italian
Copyright © 1999 ITL spa, Milano, Italy

Translated by Andrew Tulloch

The cover reproduces a
XIII century Icon of the Transfiguration
now venerated in the Russian Orthodox Patriarcate of Moscow

ST PAULS Publishing
187 Battersea Bridge Road
London SW11 3AS, UK

Copyright (English Translation) © ST PAULS UK 2000

ISBN 085439 589 X

Set by Tukan DTP, Fareham, UK
Produced in the EC
Printed by AGAM, Cuneo, Italy

ST PAULS is an activity of the priests and brothers of
the Society of St Paul who proclaim the Gospel
through the media of social communication

Contents

THE TRANSFIGURATION OF JESUS

Matthew 17:1-8   *Mark 9:2-8*   *Luke 9:28-36*

1. Six days later, Jesus took with him Peter and James and his brother John and led them up a high mountain, by themselves.
2. And he was transfigured before them, and his face shone like the sun, and his clothes became dazzling white.
3. Suddenly there appeared to them Moses and Elijah, talking with him.

2. Six days later, Jesus took with him Peter and James and John, and led them up a high mountain apart, by themselves.
3. And he was transfigured before them, and his clothes became dazzling white, such as no one on earth could bleach them.
4. There appeared to them Elijah with Moses, who were talking with Jesus.

28. Now about eight days after these sayings Jesus took with him Peter and John and James, and went up on the mountain to pray.
29. And while he was praying, the appearance of his face changed, and his clothes became dazzling white.
30. Suddenly they saw two men, Moses and Elijah, talking to him.
31. They appeared in glory and were speaking of his departure, which he was about to accomplish at Jerusalem.
32. Now Peter and his companions were weighed down with sleep; but since they had stayed awake, they saw his glory and the two men who stood with him.

4. Then Peter said to Jesus, "Lord, it is beautiful for us to be here; if you wish, I will make three dwellings here, one for you, one for Moses, and one for Elijah."

5. Then Peter said to Jesus, "Rabbi, it is beautiful for us to be here; let us make three dwellings, one for you, one for Moses, and one for Elijah."
6. He did not know what to say, for they were terrified.

33. Just as they were leaving him, Peter said to Jesus, "Master, it is beautiful for us to be here; let us make three dwellings, one for you, one for Moses, and one for Elijah" – not knowing what he said.

5. While he was still speaking, suddenly a bright cloud overshadowed them, and from the cloud a voice said, "This is my Son, the Beloved; with him I am well pleased; listen to him!"
6. When the disciples heard this, they fell to the ground and were overcome by fear.
7. But Jesus came and touched them, saying, "Get up and do not be afraid."

7. Then a cloud overshadowed them, and from the cloud there came a voice, "This is my Son, the Beloved; listen to him!"

34. While he was saying this, a cloud came and overshadowed them; and they were terrified as they entered the cloud.
35. Then from the cloud came a voice that said, "This is my Son, my Chosen; listen to him !"

8. And when they looked up, they saw no one except Jesus himself alone.

8. Suddenly when they looked around, they saw no one with them any more, but only Jesus.

36. When the voice had spoken, Jesus was found alone. And they kept silent and in those days told no one any of the things they had seen.

Introduction

As I begin this pastoral letter, which I hope will help both myself and the faithful of my diocese to experience the passing of the millennium in its fullness, I feel that there are many themes, too many even, that are knocking at the door of my heart. I will try to mention at least the principal ones.

In this year 2000, which stands on the threshold between two centuries and two millennia, while remembering the gift which was the incarnation of God's Son twenty centuries ago, I would like to reflect first of all on *the meaning of time and of history* and of the events that unfold within them. I find myself asking certain questions. At what point have we arrived on the human journey? As believers how have we welcomed the gift of God, the Lord Jesus, so far? What meaning can we give the new millennium? These questions take on a particular importance and urgency against the background of recent events in the Balkan war and of the ethnic hatred that this has so forcibly brought to light: how is it possible that the twentieth century can end with such dramatic events, as if nothing had been learnt from the tragic lessons of the two World Wars, from the genocides perpetrated and from the fall of ideological systems?

The Pope asks us to reflect on history and the events we see unfolding before our eyes in the light of the *mystery of the Trinity,* a mystery which lies at the very heart of Christian revelation. He asks that the year 2000, following on from the three-year period dedicated to the Son Jesus, the Spirit and the Father, be dedicated to the praise of the Trinity *(Tertio Millenio Adveniente,* No. 55). But what does it mean to contemplate this mystery from which everything comes and to which everything tends? How can this mystery help us to live the ending of our century and the millennium with a touch of optimism and serenity?

We live in the *Western World,* characterised by apathy and weariness. This apathy and weariness manifests itself particularly, in society, through the declining birth rate, and, in the Church, through the vocations crisis. What can lift us up, help us change gear, give us an horizon of joy and hope?

Everything that we do should also help to breathe life into the numerous individual projects that are being prepared and promoted in view of the *Great Jubilee* on a global, national, regional and diocesan level. Our projects should not remain a mixture of unconnected gatherings and activities. We must see them as all forming part of a journey of repentance and conversion, a journey that we experience as a radiant moment in the great pilgrimage of humanity to the Father.

Prompted by such a great number of things to consider, I searched long and hard, together with various diocesan Councils, for a word that would somehow summarise these concerns, provide an icon to draw them all together. During this search, as I sometimes agonised over the great number of themes and the difficulty of linking them together in a convincing way, I found the question that Dostoyevsky placed on the lips of one of the characters in his novel *The Idiot,* increasingly present in my heart. The atheist Ippolit asks Prince Myshkin, "'Is it true, Prince, that you once said that the world will be saved by 'beauty' ? Gentlemen," he shouted in a loud voice to all the company, "the prince says that the world will be saved by beauty!... What sort of beauty will save the world?¹'" The Prince did not respond to the question (like the day when the Nazarene standing before Pilate responded to the question, 'What is truth?' (Jn 18:38) simply by his presence).

It almost seems that the silence of Myshkin – who stood, with the infinite compassion of love, next to the youth who was dying of consumption at eighteen years of age tells us that the ***beauty that will save the world is the love that shares the pain***.

The beauty of which I speak is not therefore the seductive beauty which actually distances us from the true goal, that goal which our restless hearts seek. This beauty is rather the 'Beauty so ancient and so new', that Augustine confesses is the object of his love purified by his conversion, the beauty of God[2]; it is the beauty which characterises the Shepherd who guides us with firmness and tenderness along the ways of God, and who is called in John's Gospel 'the beautiful Shepherd, who lays down his life for his sheep' (Jn 10:11). It is the beauty which Francis of Assisi refers to when he invokes the Eternal saying, in his *Praises of God Most High,* 'You are beauty'. It is the beauty that the Pope wrote about recently in his *Letter to Artists* affirming, 'In perceiving that all he had created was good, God saw that it was beautiful as well... In a certain sense, beauty is *the visible form of the good,* just as the good is the *metaphysical condition of beauty*' (No. 3). It is the beauty before which 'the soul experiences a certain noble elevation of the spirit above and beyond the simple predisposition to pleasure of the senses' (Immanuel Kant, *The Critique of Pure Reason*, §59). We are not talking, therefore, of a quality which is only exterior and 'conventional' but of that experience which can be described using terms such as 'glory' (the biblical word which best expresses the 'beauty' of God insofar as it is revealed to us), 'splendour' and 'fascination'. It is that which arouses joyous attraction, pleasant surprise, which causes us to feel ardent devotion, to fall in love, to be enthusiastic. It is that beauty which love discovers in the person who is loved, that person who – as we grasp intuitively – is worthy of the gift of ourselves, for whom we are ready to step out of ourselves and to risk everything readily.

I feel that the question which *this* beauty still provokes today is: 'What beauty will save the world?' It is not enough to deplore the ugliness that fills our world. Neither is it enough, in our 'disincarnated' age, to talk of justice, duties, the common good, pastoral programmes, and the demands of the Gospel.[3] We must talk with a heart full of compassionate love, experiencing that charity which gives with joy and enkindles the enthusiasm of all it touches. We must

13

radiate the beauty of that which is *true* and *just* in life, because only this beauty truly captivates the heart and turns it to God. In short, we must understand what Peter understood when he saw Jesus transfigured, 'Lord, it is beautiful for us to be here' (Mt 17:4), and what Paul, quoting Isaiah (52:7), felt when faced with the task of announcing the Gospel, 'How beautiful are the feet of those who bring good news!' (Rom 10:15).

Our time appears to us full of ugly and distressing things. But those who know they are loved by God, and who make an effort to keep this faithful and reciprocal love alive in the various situations that the trials of life and history throw them into, can see beyond them. Such people find real beauty in life at the turn of the millennium, and try to understand our age, with all the painful and disturbing enigmas that it presents to us. It is a beautiful thing to search for the signs of Trinitarian love in history; it is a beautiful thing to follow Jesus and to love his Church; it is a beautiful thing to read the world and our lives in the light of the Cross; it is a beautiful thing to give our life for our brothers and sisters! It is a beautiful thing to stake our own existence on he who is not only the truth in person, not only the greatest good, but the only one who reveals to us the divine beauty for which our hearts have a profound longing and intense need.

Now we can turn to the icon which I referred to earlier in this pastoral letter. The icon is that of the Transfiguration, and it links together all that we have been saying so far:

— in the disciples who *ascend the mountain,* carrying in their hearts all the anxieties and burdens that agitate them, both personally and collectively, we can read the questions that we ourselves ask regarding the meaning of time, and the demand for meaning arising from the anguish which the violence and all the tragic events of our twentieth century produces;

— in the disciples who *on the mountain live* the beautiful experience of the revelation of the Father and the beloved Son and the Spirit in the cloud we can begin to grasp how these pressing questions and the Trinitarian mystery are related, for the relationship between the two is able to meet the need we have to understand the basic and underlying reasons for our journey in the faith;

— in the disciples who *descend the moun- tain,* they themselves transfigured in heart, we can see the need we all of us have to go and live our lives of faith, our pastoral activities, and in particular any Jubilee projects we may be participating in, with resolution and a sincere desire for conversion and renewal.

This letter, therefore, is designed first of all as a meditation on the Transfiguration, which we will consider as three separate 'moments': the ascent of the mountain, the revelation on the mountain, and the descent from the mountain. Dominating all this is, of course, the theme of the beauty of the revelation of the Trinity. This theme is prominent in the Synoptic accounts of the Transfiguration (Mt 17:1-10; Mk 9:2-8; Lk 9:28-37), all three of which have been laid out alongside each other at the beginning of this book.

NOTES

1. Dostoyevsky, F., *The Idiot*. Translated by D. Magarshack. Penguin Books, London, 1955, Part III, chapter V, p. 394.

2. Augustine, *Confessions,* Translated by R.S. Pine-Coffin. Penguin Books, London, 1961, 10,27, p.231.

3. 'In a world without beauty (even if people cannot manage without this word and have it always on their lips, misunderstanding its meaning), in a world perhaps not deprived of it but no longer able to see it, to make it part of their calculations, even goodness has lost its

power to attract, the evidence of the fulfilment of its *'devoir-etre'*. The human person remains perplexed before goodness, and asks themselves why they should not prefer evil. [...] In a world that does not believe itself capable anymore of affirming the good, the arguments in favour of the truth have lost their logical force' (H. Urs von Balthasar, *Perception of the Forms,* translated from the Italian edition, volume 1 of *Gloria,* Milano, 1985, 11). All of von Balthasar's trilogy, beginning with the seven volumes of *Glory* and then in the *Theodrama* and *Logic* deepens this understanding of the mystery of God from the point of view of the 'beautiful', and of the perfect expression the 'beautiful' finds in the Incarnate Word and in the Church working in history.

Our Programme:
a Prologue

At this point I am ready to enter into the discussion of the actual subject of this Pastoral Letter, but there is still something which holds me back. I ask myself: how can I enable those who will read this letter to share in all the research and hard work that went into its writing? How can we deepen our understanding of the Trinity, which is the aim of this letter, and thereby turn it into a true spiritual experience? A clear exposition of doctrine of the sort that can be found in all the catechisms[1], is not sufficient for this purpose. The mystery of the Trinity asks that we enter deeply into it, even to the point of accepting suffering.

There are in fact different ways of approaching the mystery of the Trinity. The classical approach considers God from the point of view of his mystery as unity in multiplicity; it studies the relations between the Persons of the Trinity, and sees this 'multiplicity-communion' reflected in certain ways in the human community, starting with the family. In this approach the Trinity appears as a model for relations between people, and can be used to form the basis of a correct understanding of society and, above all, of the Church.

More usual today is the 'salvation history' approach: the Trinity progressively reveals itself in the events that bring about our salvation, the centre of which is the Incarnation. God reveals himself as Father in sending the Son; in his self-abandonment to the Father and the Father's will until death, the Son reveals his unity with the Father; the Spirit is given by the Son and continues the Son's presence among humankind. Thus, in the mystery of Easter, God appears as Father, Son and Holy Spirit.

While thinking about these different approaches, which do not exclude each other but are complementary, I felt the need to take a more personal approach to the subject, a way of understanding that is almost instinctive. A sort of knowledge of God that requires us to take a step forward in faith-hope-charity, that costs something, that marks an overcoming of self through which room is created for knowing God. A knowledge that provides a key to understanding

– obtained at a high price (cf 1 Cor 6:20; 7:23) – time and the meaning of all that happens to humanity, and helps us to understand as well our own selves and the 'us today' of the Church. If it is true that a purely 'objective' knowledge of God is not possible, but that he can be known only by entering into a relationship with him and giving oneself, the 'way of entry' is Jesus, who loves and gives himself without regret.

What this means, therefore, is that entry into the mystery of the Trinity begins with the Son, and with a spiritual 'step forward' that involves the whole person. Jesus himself said, 'no one knows the Father except the Son and anyone to whom the Son chooses to reveal him' (Mt 11:27). We must, therefore, enter into the experience of the Son.

This experience of the Son expresses itself above all in two moments: in gratitude and abandonment. The moment of gratitude is expressed in verses like Matthew 11:25: 'At that time Jesus said, "I thank you, Father, Lord of heaven and earth"'; or like John 11:41: 'And Jesus looked upward and said, "Father, I thank you for having heard me."' This means we can participate in the gratitude of Jesus who receives everything from his Father, and finds a way to praise him in everything. By living the spirit of gratitude and of filial joy for all we receive, even if it is contrary to our expectations, we enter into that knowledge that Jesus had of the Father and in him live something of the mystery of the Trinity.

The moment of abandonment is expressed in passages like Matthew 26:39: 'not what I want but what you want', and like Luke 23:46: 'Father, into your hands I commend my Spirit', read in the light of Matthew 27:46:4: 'My God, My God, why have you forsaken me?' These moments witness the supreme expression of Jesus' absolute faith in his Father, the Father who he feels has abandoned him. By entering intimately into the heart of Christ we are enabled to say that we know the Father better through the feelings experienced by the Son. There are moments in life when such an experience requires heroic dedication. In these moments we feel more clearly that it is not in us to live such feelings, but that it is the Spirit that arouses them inside our heart. In these moments we have entered the heart of Jesus' experience of the Father and the Spirit. In these moments the Trinity is no longer an abstract theory or an idea that emerges out of a series of tales or narratives, but something that we feel inside and that makes us resonate in harmony with the divine mystery. Such experiences create in us a spiritual 'centredness' from which it is possible to think again about all the questions we have been asking ourselves in this letter about our world and its history. Such a reassessment is not performed in order to produce yet again theoretical answers that are almost separate from our own selves, but to grasp intuitively what our involvement must be in that passion of love and compassion with which the Trinity created the world, loving it and thereby leading it to its fullness.

Every aspect of this pastoral letter has been lived, before being written. We have to let ourselves be moved by the Spirit in order to enter into the heart of the Son, and so to know the Father. This letter has been written with no other aim in mind than to help everyone complete this journey.

Now we are ready to enter into the *lectio divina* of the episode of the Transfiguration.

NOTES

1. The Cardinal refers his (Italian) readers to: Conferenza Episcopale Italiana, *La verita vi fara liberi, Catechismo degli adulti,* 1995, 165-180. In English see, *The Catechism of the Catholic Church.* Geoffrey Chapman, London, 1994, nn. 232-267, for instance.

I

What Beauty Will Save the World?

The Ascent of Tabor and the Questions of the Disciples

The apostles whom Jesus invited to ascend with him up the mountain, six days after the announcement of a forthcoming mysterious appearance of the Son of Man (cf Mt 17:1), carried with them the increasingly burdensome questions that they had been harbouring in their hearts. Standing next to Jesus and learning to compare their previous vision of life and of history with what he did and taught, they asked themselves: in what way does this Master, who exercises such a great fascination, live up to God's promises for the salvation of his people? How can a man who is so good and gentle put to rights a world that is so bad? And what does it mean when he talks about the destiny of defeat and death? (cf Mt 16:21-23).

These are the very questions that we Christians find ourselves asking at the end of this century and of this millennium: how can the gentle beauty of the Crucified One who has risen, bring salvation to this cynical and cruel humanity?

This is the question that Dostoyevsky put in the mouth of Ippolit a century ago, and that re-echoes today in different forms; for example:

— on the grand stage of history, where the Balkan war has reopened wounds that in Europe at least were thought to have been healed for good;
— in the difficulty and weariness that one often notices that those who believe experience when they try to give a reason, with enthusiasm and conviction, for the hope that is within them in the face of the evil of the world;
— in the discouragement that tempts everyone a little when they are faced with the banality of everyday life and the many types of ugliness encountered in life, coupled with an inability to see in all the banal and distressing things we encounter a call to something greater, something for which it might be worth spending yourself.

a. Vision of the Times: Not a 'Brief Century' any longer

The events of 1999 in the Balkans seem to stand in contradiction to the opinion expressed by some, that the twentieth century was the 'brief century' (Eric Hobsbawm), i.e. a century which was concluded by the prophetic year of 1989. All the atrocities of the twentieth century that seemed unrepeatable, have returned: war, genocide, destruction and death. The century that seemed to close with the crisis of the ideologies (such as Communism or Fascism) now finds itself marked by ideological divisions and conflicts comparable to those of the two World Wars or the long decades of the cold war: in this sense we can say that ours is not the predicted 'brief Century'. Our century is the century in which ideologies once believed to be vanquished, in reality continue to influence the decisions of individuals and peoples with their logic of conflict, producing new and terrible acts of violence. We know, of course, that what happened in the Balkans is only one example of the numerous tragedies that marked many other countries, above all in Africa.

As we enter the threshold of the Jubilee Year – that we are invited to live in contemplation of the course of history in the light of the Trinity – it seems, therefore, that the perennial anguished questions, which are deeply rooted in human suffering, are repeating themselves once again: what meaning is there in history, in the endless sequence of humanity's actions? How does God reveal himself in the tragedies of history? Why does the Father of mercies seem to remain silent in the face of the suffering of all his creatures? Why does he allow such hatred and violence to emerge between his creatures?

b. *The Human Heart: the Difficulty of Blending Salvation and History*

What really seems to dominate our thinking about our faith is the effort to marry the today of human suffering with the today of God the Saviour, whose birth in time two thousand years ago is marked by the Jubilee. If we wish to understand the significance of these twenty centuries, whose potential for tragedy seems to be summed up by the recent wars, we must look for enlightenment to the revelation of Trinitarian love fulfilled in the Crucified One's Easter of resurrection. Easter reveals the meaning of history: history is orientated to the final victory of God, of which the resurrection of the Crucified One is a promise and an anticipation. Nevertheless, it seems that believers still experience difficulty in giving reasons for the hope that is within them (cf 1 Pet 3:15).

For this reason we need urgently to listen to God's word of closeness and of consolation, revealed at Easter: it was at Easter that God so loved the world that he gave his only Son (cf Jn 3:16); it was at Easter that the Father revealed himself as love in the supreme gesture of the sacrifice of Jesus (cf 1 Jn 4:8). Faced with this love each one of us can make their own the words of Peter on the mountain, when he witnessed the revelation of the Trinity: 'It is beautiful that we are here.' In this love revealed on the Cross we can recognise and show to all – both to believers and non-believers who are searching for meaning – the beauty that saves, which offers itself as light and strength in the confusion and suffering of our present time.

It is in the 'contemplation' of the Easter mystery that I perceive a 'code', a key to understanding my episcopal journey during these twenty years. In my twenty years as a bishop I have tried to practise contemplating both history in the light of the Trinity, and the presence of the Trinity in the interweaving of this world's events.

c. The Denial of Beauty and the Question of the Meaning of Life and of History

The intensity of our search for the beauty of God revealed at Easter is also prompted by its opposite: namely the denial of beauty. True beauty is denied wherever evil seems to triumph, everywhere violence and hatred usurp the place of love, and oppression the place of justice. But true beauty is also denied where there is no longer joy, especially where the believer's heart seems to be overwhelmed by the evidence of the evil, where enthusiasm for the life of faith is lacking and the person no longer radiates the ardour of one who believes in and follows the Lord of history.

It is true that at this point some readers of good will might say: I do wish to love the Lord, but how can I be sure that I will radiate his love? There are times that the physical, psychological and spiritual sufferings that weigh heavily on us leave us feeling anything but filled with the joy of the Gospel. Nevertheless, anyone who knows how to read the human heart, is able to perceive the deep peace underneath the suffering. Such a peace is the silent witness to the meaning of a life that is given to Christ.

The kind of denial of beauty, however, that I am speaking of here is different. This denial is often subtle and persuasive and is found in the lives of believers and non believers: such denial is found in the mediocrity that gradually creeps in, in the selfish calculations that take the place of generosity, in the repetitive and empty habits that substitute the faithfulness which ought to be lived as a continual renewal of both our heart and our life. As believers, we should ask ourselves if the Church which we build every day, is beautiful and capable of radiating God's beauty. Those who are committed to mutual fidelity in married love should ask themselves if something of the beauty of their reciprocal self-giving shines through, beyond the inevitable burdens that life brings with it. Priests and those in consecrated life, too, should ask themselves if at times habit or the ever-present disillusions have not stifled the enthusiasm they felt at the beginning. No denial of beauty is as sad as that which comes from those who have been called with their entire life to witness to the crucified love and thus to be apostles of the Beauty which saves.

Before concluding this first section I would like to mention another question that I feel welling up in my heart. What are the conditions in which our youngsters and adolescents are called today to understand something of the beauty of God and of the life lived according to the Gospel? How can they, in a consumer-oriented world, in which it seems possible to buy everything with money, not allow themselves to be deceived by what is short-lived and opt instead for something which is worthwhile and asks for sacrifice? How can they be made to understand that the vocation to beauty includes a courageous ascesis of both the heart and the mind? I am convinced that the 'beautiful witness' (cf Tim 16:13) of he who gave his life for everyone of us, which is reflected in the pages of the Scriptures, assimilated in *lectio divina* and incarnated in the lives of many witnesses of our time (from Father Maximilian Kolbe to Mother Teresa of Calcutta), is still today able to overcome all the conditioning that our age imposes on us and to give us a real enthusiasm for the true beauty of God.

II

Revelation of the Beauty that Saves

Transfiguration, Trinity and Easter Mystery

In the company of the three disciples, then, we have ascended up the mountain with Jesus, carrying along with us our questions and theirs. What will the Lord's answer be? In fact, Jesus does not speak to us: he is transfigured! 'Six days later, Jesus took with him Peter and James and John, and led them up a high mountain apart, by themselves. And he was transfigured before them, and his clothes became dazzling white, such as no one on earth could bleach them. And there appeared to them Elijah with Moses, who were talking with Jesus. Then Peter said to Jesus, 'Rabbi, it is beautiful for us to be here; let us make three dwellings, one for you, one for Moses, and one for Elijah' (Mk 9:2-5). Luke's account tells us

in addition that Moses and Elijah partici-
pated in the beauty of Jesus: 'They appeared
in glory and were speaking of his departure, which he was about to accomplish at
Jerusalem' (Lk 9:31).

In the Bible the mountain is the place of
revelation, a new Sinai where God speaks to
his people. Jesus is the Law in person, the
Torah made flesh, that reveals itself in the
splendour of the divine light: he is the living
Truth, attested to by the two witnesses *par
excellence,* Moses and Elijah who represent
the Law and the Prophets. To the disciples
this experience seems not only true and good
but also beautiful. They have experienced
the fascination of the Truth and of Goodness,
they have experienced the beauty of God
offering itself to them. This Beauty is link-
ed in the narrative with the mysterious
revelation of the Trinity: 'Then a cloud
overshadowed them, and from the cloud
there came a voice, "This is my Son, the
Beloved; listen to him"' (Mk 9:7). The cloud
and the shadow represent the Spirit of God.
The voice is that of the Father, and Jesus is
shown to be the Son, the Beloved: it is the
Trinity, therefore, that is communicating
with the disciples. The Beauty that Peter's
exclamation refers to, then, is that of the
divine Trinity.

Luke's account says explicitly that the full

revelation of the Trinity will be accomplished in the events of Easter: 'They appeared in glory and were speaking of his departure, which he was about to accomplish at Jerusalem' (Lk 9:31). In the accounts found in the other Synoptic Gospels these happenings are alluded to during the descent: 'As they were coming down the mountain, Jesus ordered them, "Tell no one about the vision until after the Son of Man has been raised from the dead". They observed the warning faithfully, though among themselves they discussed what "rising from the dead" could mean. And the disciples asked him, "Why, then, do the scribes say that Elijah must come first?" He replied, "Elijah is indeed coming and will restore all things; but I tell you that Elijah has already come, and they did not recognise him, but they did to him whatever they pleased. So also the Son of Man is about to suffer at their hands"' (Mt 17:9-12).

In the death and resurrection of the Son of Man, therefore, the Trinity definitively reveals itself as the love which saves: 'In this is love, not that we loved God but that he loved us and sent his Son to be the atoning sacrifice for our sins' (1 Jn 4:10).

The Transfiguration allows us, then, to recognise in the revelation of the Trinity the revelation of 'glory', and points us to the full realisation of this revelation in the supreme handing over of love that was fulfilled on the Cross. In this handing over the 'most beautiful of the sons of men' (cf Ps 44:3) offered himself as 'a man of suffering... from whom others hide their faces' (Is 53:3). Beauty is Love crucified, revelation of the divine heart that loves: of the Father who is the source of every gift, of the Son who was handed over to death for love of us, of the Spirit which unites Father and Son and is poured out over the human race in order to lead those who are far from God into the abyss of divine charity.

Let us accompany the disciples on the journey that Jesus showed them on the mountain: let us contemplate with them the glory of God, the divine beauty of the Cross and Resurrection of the Son of Man, and walk with them through Good Friday – the hour of darkness in which the Beauty is crucified – and carry on until we reach the splendour of Easter Day.

I would like this journey not to be merely a succession of cross-references from the Bible, but to become a path of fire, on which we advance with personal commitment and in fear and trembling, allowing ourselves to be consumed by the flame of God.

a. Beauty Crucified: Good Friday and the Today of Human Suffering

The Cross is the revelation of the Trinity in the hour of the 'handing over' and abandonment: the Father is the one who hands the Son over to death for our sake; the Son is he who hands himself over for love of us; the Spirit is the Comforter in the abandonment, whom the Son hands over to the Father in the hour of the Cross – 'Then he bowed his head and gave up his Spirit.' (Jn 19:30; cf Heb 9:14) – and the Father hands over to the Son in the resurrection (cf Rom 1:4). On the Cross suffering and death enter into God because of his love for those without God: the divine suffering, the presence of death in God, the weakness of the All-powerful are all revelations of his love for humankind. It is this love, at once unbelievable and gentle, attractive and which draws us into itself and fascinates us, that expresses the true Beauty that saves. This love is a consuming fire to those who do not resist it with an obstinate unbelief or with a persistent refusal to place themselves in silence before its mystery, that is, with the rejection of the 'contemplative dimension of life'.

This is the response the Christian God gives to the question why there is suffering in the world. It is no mere theoretical answer. God simply offers himself as the 'guardian', the 'bosom' of this grief. God does not allow a single one of his children's tears to be lost, because he makes these tears his own. He is a God who is close, who in his very closeness reveals his merciful love and his faithful tenderness. He invites us to enter into the heart of the Son who abandons himself to the Father, and thus to feel ourselves to be inside the very mystery of the Trinity.

The Son is the great companion of humanity in its suffering, and we can recognise his face in all those who suffer, above all in those whose sufferings we call 'innocent': think how strong the motive of 'innocent suffering' was in the tireless work of a Don Carlo Gnocchi for the 'disabled'. The face 'from whom others hide their faces' (Is 53:3) appears to us as a beautiful face, one which Mother Teresa of Calcutta contemplated with tenderness in the poor and dying.

b. The Splendour of Beauty: Easter and the Salvation of the World

At Easter the Beauty that saves shines out, divine charity is poured out on the world. In the Risen One, who is filled by the Father with the Spirit of life, the victory over the silence of death is fulfilled and the new humanity revealed (humanity in its fullness according to God's plan). At the same time, the supreme 'exodus' from God to humankind and from humankind to God is completed, and an opening is created to something beyond the self, which the human heart longs for. If we make the happenings of Easter ours in faith, we too will be swept away by this whirlwind which invites us to come out of ourselves, to forget ourselves, to taste the beauty inherent in the act of the 'free gift of self'.[1]

c. Encounter with the Beauty that Saves: the Apparition Accounts

The revelation of the Trinity as divine beauty that saves, reaches the lives of the disciples in the meetings described in the biblical accounts of the apparition of the Risen Jesus to his disciples. Though the scenes differ from each other in time and place, there is a recurrent structure common to all: in every scene it is the Risen One who takes the initiative, and he shows himself to be living (cf Acts 1:3). The encounters that the disciples had with the Risen One, become, through the words and gestures used in the Church's liturgy, our encounters with the same Risen Lord. As they did for the disciples, these words and gestures arouse in us a joyful surprise, exultation because of the glory of the Risen One, consolation in feeling ourselves so loved, the will to give ourselves to him who calls us to participate in his fullness of life, and the desire to shout out the joyful confession of faith: 'It is the Lord!' (Jn 21:7), 'My Lord and my God' (Jn 20:28).

Those who have encountered the Risen One are sent by him to be his witnesses: the Easter encounter transforms the life of anyone who experiences it. The cowardly fugitives of Good Friday become the courageous witnesses of Easter, so much so that they give their lives in order to confess their Lord. His splendour truly enraptured their hearts and turned them into announcers of the gift of God. Those who have experienced salvation and tasted its beauty and joy, experience an uncontainable need to take the gift they have received to others.

Transfigured by the love that saves, the disciples become witnesses to this transfiguration: the beauty that has enraptured them, drives them to give freely to all that which was freely given to them.

d. The 'Beautiful Shepherd' and the Church of Love

Being a witness to the Beauty which saves is something that is born from the continual and ever new experience of this Beauty: Jesus makes us understand this when, in the Gospel of John, he presents himself as the 'beautiful Shepherd' (so it is in the original Greek, even if translations normally prefer 'good shepherd'): 'I am the beautiful shepherd. The beautiful shepherd lays down his life for the sheep... I am the beautiful shepherd. I know my own and my own know me, just as the Father knows me and I know the Father. And I lay down my life for the sheep' (Jn 10:11, 14-15). The beauty of the shepherd lies in the love with which he hands himself over to death for each one of his sheep and establishes with each one of them a direct and personal relationship of the most intense love. This means that we experience his beauty by allowing ourselves to be loved by him, handing over our own hearts to him so that he can flood them with his presence, and returning this love which we have received in this way with the love that Jesus himself renders us capable of possessing.

The place where this encounter of beautiful and vivifying love with the

Shepherd is possible, is the Church: in the Church the beautiful Shepherd speaks to the hearts of each one of his sheep and makes the gift of his life for us present in the sacraments. In the Church the disciples can nourish themselves on the Word, on the sacraments and on the charity lived in community, receiving from these sources the joy of knowing themselves loved by God and protected with Christ in the heart of the Father. In this sense the Church is a Church of Love, a community of the Beauty that saves. To be part of this community with the total adherence of a heart that believes and loves, is an experience of joy and beauty that nothing and no one in the world can give in the same way. To be called to serve this Church with the whole of one's being in the priesthood or consecrated life is a beautiful and precious gift, and one that makes us exclaim 'The boundary lines have fallen for me in pleasant places; I have a goodly heritage' (Ps 16:6).

Confirmation of this comes from the lives of the Saints: not only did they believe in the 'beautiful Shepherd' and love him, but above all they let themselves be loved and shaped by him. The charity of the 'beautiful Shepherd' becomes theirs; his beauty is poured out in their hearts and radiated by their actions.

When the Church of Love lives in full its identity as a community gathered together by the 'beautiful Shepherd' in divine charity, it offers itself as a living 'icon' of the Trinity and announces the beauty that saves the world. This is the Church that has generated us in the faith and continually makes our hearts beautiful with the light of the Word, the forgiveness of God and the strength of the bread of life. This is the Church that we would like to be, a Church in which we open ourselves to the splendour that radiates from above, so that this splendour – dwelling in our communities – might attract the 'pilgrimage of the nations'. This pilgrimage is that which was foreseen in the marvellous vision that the Prophets had of the final salvation: 'In days to come the mountain of the Lord's house shall be established as the highest of the mountains, and shall be raised above the hills; all the nations shall stream to it. Many peoples shall come and say, "Come let us go up to the mountain of the Lord, to the house of the God of Jacob; that he may teach us his ways and that we may walk in his paths"' (Is 2:13; cf Mic 4:1-3; Zech 8:20; 14:16; Is 56:6-8; 60:11-14). Through his people the 'beautiful Shepherd' will be able to reach many with the light of salvation. Thus many will be attracted to him, and his beauty will save the world.

NOTES

1. The beauty of Easter is at the same time integral, harmonious and clear: in it, therefore, are found the three aspects of beauty that the classical tradition has always underlined. St Thomas affirms *(Summa Theologica* I q. 39a. 8c): *'Pulchritudo* habet similitudinem cum propriis Filii', 'Beauty has a likeness to the property of the Son'. St Thomas adds an explanation of this idea that these three aspects must be present for something to be beautiful: 'integrity' or 'perfection' *(integritas),* 'proportion' or 'harmony' *(proportio)* and 'brightness' or 'clarity' *(claritas).* The Angelic Doctor recognises the presence of these three elements in the Son: in particular, the 'all' or 'whole' of the divinity makes itself present and shines out in the 'fragment', which is the humanity of the Saviour. In Jesus, beauty appears insofar as he – perfect icon of the Father – is the revelation of the divine mystery that makes itself known and loved amongst us, and, at the same time, insofar as he is the door that opens onto the abyss of Trinitarian love and communicates this love to us. (cf *Summa Theologica.* Translated by the Fathers of the English Dominican Province. Copyright © 1947 Benzinger Brothers Inc.).

   As John Paul II writes in his *Letter to Artists,* 'In becoming man, the Son of God has introduced into human history all the evangelical wealth of the true and the good, and with this he has also unveiled a new dimension of beauty, of which the Gospel message is filled to the brim' (No. 5).

III
Witnesses to the Beauty that Saves

The Descent from the Mountain and the Invitation

'Get up and do not be afraid'

The disciples respond to the gift of the Transfiguration by trying to capture the beauty that they experienced: 'Just as they were leaving him, Peter said to Jesus, "Master, it is beautiful for us to be here; let us make three dwellings, one for you, one for Moses, and one for Elijah" – not knowing what he said"' (Lk 9:33). Beauty however is not possessed, it is a gift and as such must be given, not kept back: the disciples prostrate in adoration and seized by a great fear are approached and touched by Jesus who says to them: 'Get up and do not be afraid' (Mt 17:7). Jesus invites them to take up the journey again without fear, to descend the mountain towards ordinary life and to embark upon the great road that will bring the Son of Man to Jerusalem for him to fulfil his destiny.

This invitation is addressed also to us. We are invited to continue on our pilgrimage to the heavenly Jerusalem without fear, knowing that he is with us and that for this reason, life is beautiful and that it is beautiful to commit ourselves to the Kingdom. We are invited to welcome, announce and share with all the Beauty that saves. If we wished to make this thought relevant for today, we would say that rediscovering the beauty of God means rediscovering the reasons for our faith when faced with the evil that devastates the earth, and the profound reasons for our commitment to serve all, for the glory of God. Whoever experiences the Beauty, which appeared on Tabor and rediscovers it in the mystery of Easter, whoever believes in the announcement of the Word of faith and allows themselves to be reconciled with the Father in the communion of the Church, discovers the beauty of an existence so profound that nothing and nobody in the world can give them.

The disciple of Jesus is invited to nourish themselves on this Beauty, which comes from above, becoming continually its announcer, in order to share it with those who do not know it and with those who in different ways are searching for it. The invitation is extended to us all in a special way in this year of grace and renewal, which is the Jubilee of the Year 2000. Therefore, in the name of Jesus crucified and risen again, I want to say to all of you the word that resounds from Tabor: 'Get up and do not be afraid!' I invite you to experience the gift of God, the true beauty that saves, to proclaim it in word and in life, in order to share with all the splendour of the true and the good, which is the light of the divine Beauty.

Comforted by the icon of the Transfiguration, which has led me to contemplate with you the revelation of the Trinity and its beauty in the holy Triduum of Easter, I want to cry out with you: 'Master, it is beautiful for us to be here' (Lk 9:33; cf Mt 17:4; Mk 9:5), in the desire to find the encouragement in this experience of grace to continue our vocation and mission with an ever-increasing joy. In particular, I would like to remind my brothers in the ordained ministry of the words used by the apostle Paul to describe the task entrusted to us: 'I do not mean to imply that we lord it over your faith; rather, we are workers with you for your joy' (2 Cor 1:24). And I would like to remind all those who live the consecrated life of what John Paul II said to them, referring to this same episode of the Trans-figuration: 'Those who by the power of the Holy Spirit are led progressively into full configuration to Christ reflect in themselves a ray of the unapproachable light. During their earthly pilgrimage, they press on towards the inexhaustible Source of light. The consecrated life thus becomes a particularly profound expression of the Church as the Bride who, prompted by the Spirit to imitate her Spouse, stands before him in splendour, without spot or wrinkle or any such thing, that she might be holy and without blemish' (Eph 5:27). (Post-Synodal Apostolic Exhortation *Consecrated Life*, no. 19).

a. Experiencing the Beauty that Saves: Conversion and Reconciliation

The experience of the Beauty that saves means first of all the living of the journey of faith, especially in personal and liturgical prayer. This prayer takes place in God and in the Spirit; it comes to the Father through the Son and receives everything from him in peace. Such prayer is the experience of knowing oneself to be loved and saved, irrevocably entrusted to the living God, hidden with Christ in the relations of love that exist in the Trinity. We come to such an experience through conversion of heart and reconciliation with the community.

The Beauty of divine charity – once it is experienced in the depths of the heart – cannot but lead us to overcome the individualism which is unfortunately widespread even among Christians. We are led to rediscover the value of the 'we' in our lives, as much on the level of the Church community as on that of individual family communities, and in all the ways in which we as believers find ourselves living in relation to others. In particular, the beauty of communion should shine out in the communities of those who live the consecrated life. The brothers and sisters who live in these communities are called by their vocation to let their communities be an icon of the communion that exists in all the Church, a communion founded on that of the divine Trinity.

The beauty of communion should shine out also in the liturgy. Just think of how important it is for a liturgical celebration to reflect something of the beauty of the mystery of God in its seasons, gestures, words, and furnishings!

Every time, in the heart of the Eucharistic celebration, when the splendour of the truth manifests itself to those in prayer, the exclamation 'mystery of the faith' wells up from their conscious wonder. When we have done what the Lord Jesus commanded the Apostles to do 'in memory of him', the eyes of faith are opened, like those of the disciples on the road to Emmaus (cf Lk 24:30-31), and we confess the 'mystery of mercy' (cf 1 Tim 3:16) with wonder and gratitude. The Beauty which saves, unveils itself in the mystery of Christ, culminating with Easter: the Eucharistic celebration is its memorial. The need to celebrate the liturgy well and with beauty is well rooted in these convictions. The rhythm of words, silence, singing, music and actions in the unfolding of the liturgical rite all contribute to this spiritual experience.[1]

b. Announcing the Beauty that Saves

In this last stretch of the century and millennium the encounter with Beauty gives a new life to the missionary impetus in all its forms: the proclamation of the Beauty of the divine Trinity, the preparation of those who wish to experience this Beauty, the witness to charity and the commitment to justice that derives from it, the forming of young people in these values – all are tasks which require the 'descent from the mount'.

The Jubilee 'itinerary' lends itself particularly well to the living of this announcement of the Beauty that saves with its five 'moments': spiritual, ecclesial, charitable, penitential and Marian.[2]

But art, too, is an announcement of the Beauty that saves. 'Every genuine inspiration, however, contains some tremor of that "breath" with which the Creator Spirit suffused the work of creation from the very beginning. Overseeing the mysterious laws governing the universe, the divine breath of the Creator Spirit reaches out to human genius and stirs its creative power. He touches it with a kind of inner illumination which brings together the sense of the good and the beautiful, and he awakens energies of mind and heart which enable it to conceive an idea and give it form in a work of art. It is right then to speak, even if only analogically, of "moments of grace", because the human being is able to experience in some way the Absolute who is utterly beyond' (John Paul II, *Letter to Artists,* No. 15).

At this point I would like to underline in particular the significance of architecture and sacred iconography. When these arts are born from the 'mark' that beauty leaves on its beholder, then they are true to their primary function: witnessing the breaking-in of the divine into our day-to-day existence.

Out of date and repetitive Church architecture and iconography that make no effort
to respect rules are not able to stir up the
emotion which belongs to the mystery por-
trayed by them, they do not move us and do
not lead us to praise. These arts should be
an arrow launched at our inner being
through the language of beauty, something
which acts as an aid to contemplation.

c. *Sharing with All the Search for and the Gift of Beauty*

If we would listen to the true demands of
the human heart then we must treasure
every longing for beauty, wherever it is
present, in order to journey with everyone
in search of the Beauty that saves. A true
commitment to ecumenism, inter-religious
and inter confessional dialogue is urgently
needed if we are to respect and promote
Beauty as we do justice, peace and the
safeguarding of creation. We must here learn
to value the experience of dialogue with non-
believers. This dialogue could act as a form
of common search for the Beauty that saves.

Sharing the gift of Beauty means moreover
that we must live the gratuitousness of love:
charity is the Beauty that spreads out and
transforms all who are touched by it. In

charity there is no relation of dependence between the one who gives and the one who receives, but an exchange that takes place through the shared participation in the gift of Beauty crucified and risen, in the divine Love that saves. We must discover the value of the one who is other and is different. In doing so, we model ourselves on the interrelationship between the three divine Persons: the other is not a rival or a dependent, but an enriching and grace-filled Other.

d. *Living the Jubilee Year in the Unity of the three Dimensions: Sacramental, Prophetic and Charitable*

The unity of the three dimensions here indicated – that of the sacramental experience of the Beauty that saves, that of the hearing of the Word that it announces, and that of its proclamation, the sharing of it in charity – must always be sought, but it has a particular urgency in the Jubilee Year. This unity will not come about without a fresh reading of life and of history, undertaken in the light of the Trinity; it will not come about unless we nourish ourselves on the sacraments of life, rediscovered in all their richness as places of encounter with the Beauty that saves; it will not come about unless we make a real effort to share the gift of this same Beauty with all. Liturgy and spiritual life, catechesis and evangelisation, dialogue and the service of charity will have to experience a fresh new of life in this Jubilee Year. This new surge must be fired by a fresh encounter with the Beauty of God. This beauty is to be encountered on the 'Tabor' of the journey of time which is the year 2000.[3]

NOTES

1. It is in the context of this way of renewing the experience of the Beauty that saves, encountered especially in the gift of grace that are the sacraments, that we must place the proposal to increase the value of the Liturgical Year's 'itinerary', particularly its important moments (outside the itinerary for the Jubilee itself). This proposal is aimed at helping us rediscover the beauty of God and its significance for life and for history, through conversion and penitence. (In connection with this proposal for liturgical reform the Cardinal invites his Italian readers to use instructions in the chapter 'Tool for pastoral Councils' in the title *Lavorare insieme 1999-2000* ('Working Together'), especially p. 8-13)

2. Cf *Lavorare insieme 1999-2000* (pp. 14-19).

3. The whole of *Lavorare insieme* gives useful suggestions to make the celebration of the Jubilee into a great occasion of grace, which offers everyone the opportunity to experience God's gift as a gift of reconciliation and joy.

Conclusion

Pondering God's Work in the Heart:
the Icon of the Annunciation

A biblical icon will help us to conclude our reading of this letter in the light of the mystery of Easter, which reveals the Trinity to us, and to better overcome the problems caused by the many denials of beauty that we see: the scene of the Annunciation (cf Lk 1:26-38).

Mary represents the believer who listens to the mystery of God, even when she is faced with the inscrutability of God's plan: 'Mary said to the angel, "How can this be, since I am a virgin?"' (Lk 1:34). She does not doubt: she only wants to be guided in her ways by the Lord. She is already the woman of Good Friday, whose soul is pierced by a sword (cf Lk 2:35) at the foot of her Son's Cross (cf Jn 19:25-27). She is already the Mary of Holy Saturday, the only one who keeps her faith in the hour of God's silence and his apparent defeat in the struggle with the powers of this world. And yet, she is already the woman of reconciliation, the Virgin who was covered by the shadow of the Most High in order to conceive the Word in the flesh, and who is wrapped in the relations that exist between God the Father and the Son that are present in her by the strength of the Spirit.

In everything she is close to us, in the fragility of our creaturely nature and in the sorrowful experience of accompanying her Son to the Cross. Mary is the woman who with the 'yes' of her faith made her own today into the today of God. She 'treasured all these words and pondered them in her heart' (Lk 2:19), or – as we might better translate the Greek – placed these words in relation to each other and all of them in relation to the mystery of God. In the annunciation, Mary teaches us to read our today in the light of the Trinity which enfolds her, recognising in the mystery of Easter the mysterious Beauty which illuminates our own time, the entire unfolding of the centuries, and, especially, the 2000 years that separate us from the first coming of the Eternal into time.

Through the intercession of Mary, the Virgin who listens and the Mother of Beautiful Love, let us ask for the ability to recognise in every being and every situation of life and of history the presence of the Trinitarian love of God, the guarding of all that exists. We are talking here about living a kind of contemplation that seeks to attain love. Like the contemplation Ignatius proposes in his *Spiritual Exercises* (Nos. 230-237), the contemplation we refer to aims to recognise and proclaim the presence of the God of love in everything. And God who is so present continually gives himself to us and offers himself as the ultimate reference point for every value. I have tried during my time as bishop to learn to see the presence of God with this sort of contemplative 'eye'. In so doing I was convinced that there is no greater gift that we can welcome and pass on, than the gift of the glory of God and of the 'eye' that is able to recognise and witness to this glory in every time.

Appendix

Some Questions for a Personal and Community 'Review of Life'

1. Check on 'Our Programme: a Prologue?'
(pp. 19-23)

Do I feel the desire to enter a little more deeply and personally into the mystery of the Trinity? Do I occasionally try to put myself in the heart of Christ in order to thank the Father in him and with him, and to abandon myself to the will of the Father even in moments of difficulty, relying on the grace of the Holy Spirit?

2. Check on 'The Ascent of Tabor and the Questions of the Disciples' (pp. 25-32)

What questions do I carry within me, do we carry within us at the end of millennium? Which of the questions mentioned in this chapter strike us the most? Are there other questions of a moral, social, civil or religious nature that we carry in our hearts? Do we place these questions before God in prayer so that we can receive light, or do we allow them to fester inside of us and burden us, not hoping for a response?

3. Check on 'Transfiguration, Trinity and Easter Mystery' (pp. 33-34)

Am I able to contemplate in the Crucified something of the beauty, of the love that saves? Do I find the reflection of the beauty of God in the apparitions of the Risen One that have touched my life even from baptism? Do I see only the human aspects of the Church (sometimes too human) that depress me, or do I try to see in the Church the presence of the 'beautiful Shepherd' that guides humanity towards the fullness of the Kingdom, despite all our weaknesses?

4. Check on 'Witness to the Beauty that Saves' (pp. 45-54)

Do I feel how beautiful it is to be reconciled with God, with our brothers and sisters and with the community? Do I allow myself to be seized by the joy of the announcing of the Gospel? What do I do to make my participation in the liturgy 'beautiful' and engaging (we would already have gone far if all the faithful would respond together and sing with one voice!)? What tasks for the Jubilee Year can we take upon ourselves as individuals and as a community?

Other titles by Carlo-Maria Martini
published by ST PAULS

Return to the Father
085439 563 6   63pp   £3.95

The Gifts of the Holy Spirit
with Dom Gueranger
085439 546 6   141pp   £4.99

David: Sinner and Believer
085439 322 6   187pp   £7.95

The Dove at Rest
085439 511 3   128pp   £6.50

Promise Fulfilled
085439 481 8   176pp   £7.25